SEAGULL
BOOKS
•
CELEBRATING
40 YEARS

THE PRIDE LIST

EDITED BY SANDIP ROY AND BISHAN SAMADDAR

The Pride List presents works of queer literature to the
world. An eclectic collection of books of queer stories,
poems, plays, biographies, histories, thoughts, ideas,
experiences and explorations, the Pride List does not
focus on any specific region, nor on any specific genre,
but celebrates the great diversity of LGBTQ+ lives
across countries, languages, centuries and identities,
with the conviction that queer pride comes from its
unabashed expression.

ALSO IN **THE PRIDE LIST**

JOSÉ LUIS SERRANO
Worst Thing of All Is the Light
Translated from the Spanish by
Lawrence Schimel

KO-HUA CHEN
Decapitated Poetry
Translated from the Chinese by
Wen-chi Li and Colin Bramwell

KIM HYUN
Glory Hole
Translated from the Korean by
Suhyun J. Ahn and Archana Madhavan

MICHAŁ WITKOWSKI
Eleven-Inch
Translated from the Polish
by W. Martin

CYRIL WONG
Infinity Diary

DANISH SHEIKH
Love and Reparation
A Theatrical Response to the Section 377
Litigation in India

MU CAO
In the Face of Death We Are Equal
Translated from the Chinese by
Scott E. Myers

PAWAN DHALL
Out of Line and Offline
Queer Mobilizations in '90s Eastern India

MIREILLE BEST
Camille in October
Translated from the French by
Stephanie Schechner

CYRIL WONG

Beachlight

LONDON NEW YORK CALCUTTA

Seagull Books, 2023

© Cyril Wong, 2023

ISBN 978 1 8030 9 264 5

British Library Cataloguing-in-Publication Data
A catalogue record for this book is available from the British Library

Cover designed by Sunandini Banerjee, Seagull Books, using a
drawing titled *Three Figures in Water* (1916) by Charles Demuth
(1883–1935), available in the public domain

Book typeset and designed by Seagull Books, using two drawings
by Charles Demuth, available in the public domain

Printed and bound by WordsWorth India, New Delhi, India

How to be a trustworthy
tour guide to this island's rim
we come to after city
life has lost its meaning?
Not nearly Navagio or nearer
Boracay. Waves crinkle
across a whispering cerement
of grey-green waters
breaking against overturned
kayaks, backdropping windows
of bars and restaurants.
Let us walk to discern more
than ocean. Let this beach unfold
secrets its visitors behold.

Injured sand, cajoling waves.
Such jazz
of unfinished things.
The air is full of horses—
when what is seen
cannot be corralled.
The hardened heart
is schist, is shit, is shaft
of shadow, is none
of these things.
Bridges collapse
between sight and thought;
between the clangour of me
and the silent, unwavering horizon.

Oh Chinese imperial poets
and their dipsomania, their lust
for moon, mountain, river and reed.
If Bai Juyi were reborn, he would write
of our nocturnal citizenry, bare bodies
like *clouds dispersing everywhere*,
most of us *the same moon colour*.
Drunk on coastal wind, the same desire,
we lead each other by protruding parts
closer to the water's frottage. Along
brightening sand, I misreport Qing emperor
Gaozong's poetry, deemed terrible:
One penis, another penis, and another . . .
All float into blooming reeds and disappear.

Zebra doves
huddle, cooing
inside armpits
of a seaside palm tree,
imitating us below
making arguments
about nothing, tongues
in each other's mouths
then lower orifices, before
parting without comment,
all desire as desperate
as it is brief, taking off
from here to chart atlases
of time disguised as air.

Briny humidity and this occasional drizzle
erode my canvas and easel, but water-
colour dries urgently in this heat. I paint
subjects absent from real life: a man
kisses another man in a corner there, so far away
passers-by fail to discern. A boy flounders
out at sea, dark arms thrashing ultramarine air.
Anyone who notices would remark that he is
at play. The child I still dream I am
blemishes the horizon with his dying.
One day my easel will break. My young wife
will shove my art to the back of some shelf
long after my death. Yet this old man carries on
painting what he sees: the unseen, the slowly drowning.

Fibonacci haiku
of a snail's shell
emptied out by birds
I weigh in my hand
like guilt or memory.
Sky fades to sea
like the mindlessness
of conservatism
into the mindlessness
of political correctness.
Clouds remain astonished
narratives of lives
unlived, whittling themselves
down to less than nothing.

The lovers take sweet time along the shore.
Not only them, but those who walk alone
like me: a single man. Oh look—a door!
To snap a picture, I fish for my phone.
I squat to twist the knob, as if to pry
then fall into a world where lovers fail
to meet, but lift the lid to crabs that lie
beneath its shade, quiescent and so frail
I lower their roof over their drowsing.
A girl and boy are holding hands. They pause
to point at me, maybe the door, musing
on metaphysics, root of every cause
which mailed a door to open at my feet
to nothing they would see, making me weep.

For how long has that old woman
been sitting there on the levee,
staring down at a man hunched over
and fishing at the far end—
maybe hoping to snare another grouper
or at least a jade-like parrotfish?
Morning to late evening,
she harbours no intention of leaving
even when the man is gone,
as if there were no man at all
but the memory of a man—
maybe her late husband—still fishing,
waiting for her to call him, so they may
leave together and later have fish for dinner.

Nature never deceives us, Rousseau assured,
it is we who deceive ourselves. My wife
disagrees, reminding us that we, too,
remain aspects of nature embattled with itself,
not separate from spume and spindrift. And who
claims that water is beyond subterfuge,
pooling to surround our two squatting, sand-faced kids
digging fist-shaped holes in view of a falling tide
that may change its mind and snatch them?
Complacently, we witness wakesurfing, windsurfing, thrills
locals allow themselves, forgetting 2004:
drowned beaches of Sri Lanka, India, Maldives, Aceh—
Playing with water the way we play with fire.
She shouts to come in from the swiftly encroaching sea.

What gospel between land
and ocean. What crabs
of once-young hearts scuttling
through the night of our bodies.
What mottled stone, muddied
sand, a toy spade washed
back to shore like evidence
of a Lilliputian crime. What reason
to play at prostration, as if
surrendering form to foam.
What oneness or primordial
innocence we abdicate,
peeling away from the ground.
What children we could have stayed.

Sandbars and sea grasses,
a sudden sentence of coral reef
punctuated by fanning anemones.
Then sea cucumbers, sea stars, sea urchins.
More snails, smashable snails
underfoot. Watch for the stonefish—ugly,
hollow-cheeked—those hypodermic
spines shoot neurotoxins
through naked soles. But how
unnatural to prance along this seawall
with slippers or worse, yellow rubber boots?
Careful, careful, we forget this land
spilled out from a tide
now grazing our amnesia.

Old men hang their loud birds
in cages from low branches
in a row over their heads.
This is not a tale of eunuchs
lamenting penile losses, but
actual men whose merboks, bulbuls
and thrushes sing in competition
with each other. Staccato
vespers, cooing elegies,
overlapping descants muscling
to outdo one another before
pews of indifferent waves.
This is turning out to be a parable
of men and their birds, after all.

Seven millennials carousing in a circle
on the sand could be seven youths
who grow together into adulthood in *The Waves*
by Virginia Woolf, but reborn in our century.
Percival, the most charismatic and handsome,
stands up, closely analysed in the dwindling light
by Neville, the poet of the group, as his first
unrequited love peels off his shirt
and wanders into the gathering foam. Percival
dies from an accident in the novel, so watch
as he swims so far from everyone that he vanishes,
as if for good. Then observe as Neville rises
to look for him, and not seeing him, he carries on
gazing beyond Percival, as if beyond time itself.

Milky zoetrope
moon takes its time
to exit the sky
to strike our heads
as we lean into billowing
sails of sea breezes.
Stroking my neck,
my partner jokes
that most things do not aim
to land on us. The moon
spins and hides,
as if on his command.
A palm on my back
pilots me safely into night.

Everything is minor.
Army boys on their Saturday-
morning run from here to there.
A child yells for her father
who has stopped to leer at them
before following her into the water.
Lovers squeeze hands before uncoupling.
Clarity of a horn
from across the ocean
or an expressway beyond some trees.
Nothing stays minor. Stray from the path:
sit on sand in slant rain.
Turn in no particular direction.
These waves still offer a mild applause.

Where attention
goes, love
flows
like foam
between toes.
Earth sucks
hard.
Observe
your reluctance
to tug
free, as if
unendurably.
This seduction
of burial—

Men arising by evening
shape silhouettes
bowered by spidery trees,
slaloming between puddles
of the moon's orgasm.
Congealed, faceless
chess pieces—always
checkmate, never
soulmate. The outlying sea
an orchestra of liquid caresses
we stray towards as ghosts
of ourselves after crimes
of intimacy. Strangers or aliens
to the sun, we could be anyone.

This bench might not know you
or it has known you all your life.
Repainted or replaced, how do you
begin to remember and yet it calls
you to sit and names you through
the hush of waves and coagulating sun,
the days you waited for love to show up.
Later a forgotten Amber Beacon tower
where you remember penetrating a man
or a man penetrating you and filling you
up along the staircase circling
its hard-on column, ecstasy
hailing you by your truest name
all the way up to the moon.

Pushing a grain of sand right into me
and not realizing what you were
doing and carrying on, carrying on
transforming pleasure into a pearl
of pain after penetrating me
with our swim trunks still
dangling around our knees
so precariously I hoped the rip
tides would not yank them gently off
the way rising currents kept pulling
the sandcastle of our bodies
down to itself, melting and absorbing
us back into the heaving
and ever-deepening waves.

Beach sand
clings
and does not slough
like sibilant skins
of the Sahara.
Air sticks
like last night's
ardour we rinse off
naked in seawater.
Early skylight
scrutinizes our pocks
and scars;
lowered eyes
and guiltless smiles.

Before the cops
catch us, we marry
heads underwater,
listing like twin
incestuous foetuses
in our mother's
womb. One last time—
we agree again
without speaking
without letting
these depths displace
each other's spit
and semen making
a home in our throats.

The life of desire
is a circus of the senses.
Under a tent of subjectivity,
such difference between wind
or sand in my eye. Discomfort
or pleasure. To exist before.
Beyond. Blessed regress
or transcendence. Ocean
of sound is no sound at all
when heard for long enough.
Salt on my tongue after a swim.
Elephant children climbing
on top of each other reek of fart
and barbecue. Blessed humanity.

The sea is a trillion commas,
keeping what it does not love
for long enough to let us
forget what we lost.
Regurgitate. Regurgitate.
Being an oasis to myself
in this wilderness of rock, sand
and bobbing children's heads
happens out of time.
Someone is yelling for somebody
to stop running, to walk
instead from here to there
and everywhere
before stopping, a capitulation.

Alan Kurdi, a two-year-old Syrian boy
spilled out dead on a beach
such as this, after drowning with his family.
Did the photographer try to save him
before taking his picture—is the question
I first asked. I am no refugee.
My grandparents arrived on a ship
at a different shore after my father
was born. In a different life,
their vessel could have foundered
before its bodies rayed out
in every direction and found land.
I imagine my father as a child
curled at my feet, face down in the sand.

Alas, the beauty of intelligent design.
Praise it to the child with brain cancer
or epidermolysis bullosa, whose skin
falls off, no, is painfully renewed again
and again like sand along this beach
the sea eats from and replenishes.
Praise it to the caterpillar whose body
is pumped full of eggs by wasps
then watch how the larvae drain
its juices before gnawing free from their
host. Alongside such thoughts, I admire
a woman lowering her head into the waves
before pulling out, hair sweeping back
like in a shampoo commercial or a baptism.

How interested are trees
in matters of outrage and injustice?
Should trees be cancelled
for posting pheromones
to inform of danger, dispensing
sugar through roots to those
weakest amongst them
without signalling their virtue?
A boy on the beach losing his kite
in sprawling branches of a ketapang
cries without acknowledging
its nodding, pagoda-shaped head—
how it might know and does not care
that kite will rattle in its skull forever.

In order for anything to happen
something must first take place.
Then after the happening, something
else follows the action that came
before. And so on and so forth
until (or already) our actions
make an ocean racing or pulling
against and away and towards itself
in every conceivable (and inconceivable)
direction. Turbulent action,
consequence, reaction that is
the road less travelled or the road
you think is the same road worn down
to nothing. A sea is every road, every place.

I know we just met but when you pat a dog
your palm passes right through it. I make a face
so it scampers across the sand. Surprise is hardly
surprising the longer we stay. Trust me
when I remind you: nothing ends.
The dog (no more than a puppy) shudders
between the ankles of a boy who reminds us
of ourselves at that age. Notice as he ignores
his pet to stare out across the water, a wish
for something he does not yet understand
twisting the shape of his open mouth.
Soon he remembers his animal, bending to touch it.
How he laughs—still not late for us to swim
inside that laugh! Before it gets too late.

Foreign maids and construction workers
hesitate to come here for fear
of disturbing the locals. A Bangladeshi man
asks to jerk me off behind my car. He is skilled
with his left hand. I do my best
to reciprocate, but stumble away when he asks
for my number. My wife will meet me
after her exercise on the other end of the beach.
I keep thinking of him, his jaw
vibrating when he came, as if bliss
ran like ice right through him. And wonder
how I may encounter more of such men
and where they hide, this honesty
of all our foreign bodies in the dark.

Such rocking hypnosis of the sea
convinces and convinces that pleasure
is pain, but also pleasure without pain.
Let us remain steadfast amongst
the stupid. Let us be stupid for only
so long. Paperweights of tankers and ships
keep the mind of the horizon in check.
Be the earth, forever turning its cheek
to suffer erosion, mocking rhythms
of ebb and flow, shifting attritions
of implacable time. Walk in praise
of dirigibles of clouds here one minute
gone the next. Walk in praise of earth,
the sea's unconscious derision, empty skies.

In a reality where truth is despised
when it cannot be utilized,
we are more likely to brutalize
each other than take long walks
on the beach, saying or doing
little else. What is left to do
along the blankest expanse of meaning?
We could hold hands (maybe not).
We might nod to the tempo
of waves, joggers and cyclists
surging along their tightrope lanes.
No motives impel us when we pause
to gaze in the same direction,
birdsong calling forth our names.

Sunshower. Unfinished cigarettes
stamped into sand. Wet but baking
under a white exoskeleton of sky,
we question whether this is like
a mind divided between what it envisions
and what it hides, or that contradiction
between the body and the soul, how
our spirit may be willing while the thing
that imprisons it travels its own way.
Light and rain, heat and coolness
not like parts of a whole but countries
at war. One lover demands to stay and sit
and enjoy the weather, while the other
ignores him, rises and waltzes with waves.

Such sandy,
shifting
ground
an ocean of thinking
slides, swings,
stands on
is more infinite, surely,
than what it holds
like slippery
but cupped hands
to night and day
rotating
like a singular
eyeball in its vast socket.

On another walk down a different stretch
of beach, Heraclitus reborn is doubting
and pointing at the waters, before he squats
to pick sand up by the palmful, analysing
the invisible factory of every grain, finger
by finger. He looks up at a child shaping
sandcastles so close to the waves and laughs.
But this is post-pandemic, so crazy
has become par for the course. Nobody
notices for long when he turns away now
to gaze back at the horizon. No longer
laughing or pointing, as if the present world
has defeated and dimmed his fire, which
in his mind could still be the source of all things.

Double jet streams yoking heat
and rain in place. Heat
migrates northwards from Africa. Heat
domes over parts of the US and Canada. Heat
boiled the sky orange. Equatorial heat
all we knew inviting more heat
than Singaporeans ever endured. Heat
unbroken by sea, no matter how near. Heat
as salt-soaked heaviness of heat
locking us behind wall after wall of heat
upon heat, no window to let heat
out. No droughts or fires (not yet) in spite of heat;
how lucky we pretend not to feel. Heat
wrangling us from the arms of each other's heat.

Mud floods in Pahang, Malaysia
left thousands homeless
and pointing fingers at reckless
land clearing by timber companies.
Temuan natives believed they are guardians
of the rainforest and upon failing
at their sacred duty, dragons
guarding the rivers caused mayhem
since altars of their land had been desecrated.
What dragon might we neglect to propitiate
when we fail to derail the avalanche
time becomes, sweeping us
lovers, loved ones, the collective beloved
like logs toppling down rivers and into the sea?

Do you know if you could survive on the beach
forever? Eat from a bin or cooling leftovers
at barbecue pits and tables of a hawker centre.
Pick up things you can use from a 200-metre belt
of bottles, wooden debris and household jetsam
regurgitated here by the southwest monsoon,
disgusting passing joggers picking up speed.
Hide from the police behind bushes that sever
the night's chill waiting to strangle your inner light.
Once I saw a dead pufferfish beside a dented can.
Another time a hawksbill turtle laying eggs.
I dream that when the planet becomes uninhabitable,
Singapore will be an island of trash vomited here from
everywhere. A plastic bag yawns, laughs, closes its mouth.

Jupiter, Mars, Saturn, Venus and Mercury
in a row today. The sky was not black enough
while clouds got in the way, like in a song
by Joni Mitchell. I wished I could afford
binoculars. Jupiter's first, someone pointed,
then Mars, Saturn, Venus and Mercury.
Did I spot any planet at all? Or was that a star,
a lone satellite absconding from the unruly earth?
Maybe I saw them all this early morning
and did not recognize what I had seen?
A homeless man on the beach staring up
at the sky, I close my eyes and there they all are,
perfectly arrayed—opening notes to an anthem
resounding in a bygone country playing me home.

Spiritual eternalism is the belief
that what moves the clouds, ruffles the waves
and combs the high branches
will always be there. Materialist annihilationism
insists that air is all there is and never
peer beyond that which nearly sends a fly careering
into my open mouth against its will.
Either or. Neither nor. How did we get here
between one extreme and another
and how do we stay in the unspeakability
thought and feeling make impossible?
Almost impossible. Sometimes I get it,
I do. And like that stunned fly, against my will
and better or lesser judgement, I do.

Sometimes I forget I am a wild child
abandoned on the beach
by mermaid parents who swam away
with my ninety-nine siblings. Having forgotten
how to revert to form, I cry until I stop
crying while on these feet steeped in sand
kissed by sun. Then remember my real parents
who only hit me when we were indoors
are waiting for me, along with brothers who
yank my hair and call me a fat girl.
I am a fat boy on the ground
pressing my naked back against the heat,
waiting for waves to creep up and draw my legs
together to make a tail.

Hearing a moan, I thought a woman was hurt
or being attacked in her electric-blue car
in the parking lot along the way
of my night's jogging route to the sea.
On closer glance I saw two women inside
kissing and realized that if I wandered any closer
they would see me. I kept jogging, faster, their moaning
insinuating into my faltering rhythm. When I reached
the water, suddenly bioluminescent and neon blue,
I longed to strip off my singlet, shorts and shoes
and jump in, spreading my legs to let the luciferian luciferase
fill me and light my loneliness from within with nothing
but blue—doing no such thing, instead I stood there
hugging my breasts, blueness dimming to the gasp of waves.

Anything happens on the beach.
A door might wash up to the seawall.
Neon water, a dead bird, a discarded tent.
You might meet the love of your life
that is not the love you settled for,
if circumstances were different, if you had
waited a year, maybe longer.
You might not have had the children
you have now, playing beside you on the grass.
Not that you love them any less
for thinking this way, for envisioning
the arbitrary and the possible.
This beach like a constant in your life
since you were a kid kicking ramparts in the sand.

Focus on difference
to intensify the thirst.
Reify every line
or footprint
in the sand.
I harden when you
harden in my mouth.
An ocean of your contentment
meets the ocean of my need.
You might insist
on what separates us
after our tryst on the beach,
but when we moan
we moan the same.

How urgent are every two or more seconds
of every moment, before the suffering
of withdrawal and longing?
Is there any real thing as experience
beyond directives and repetitions
of hope and memory? When knowledge
becomes knowing becomes unknowing—
why the lagoon when you may
disown your will to live the closer
you lurch towards the bottom of the ocean?
And wiggle back up for air, faint tinnitus
of panic in your ears, some trace
of celestial music. Then a long crawl to shore,
air bloating your lungs all you hope to lose.

Shock of sea-dank wind
buffeted our faces. I followed you
all the way out of trees towards reanimated
coastline. The muscled tree of your body
filled your shirt like light
flooding a bulb.
No stranger to strange appointments
in the shade, we cupped with sweaty hands
familiar parts. So kind of you
to lean in, so gratefully
I kissed you. Finishing each other off,
we forgot to trade numbers
which suited us fine. Or so I believed,
trailing home alone in a wake of wasted lust.

I dent the sand with my high heels
after fleeing the restaurant. My husband
got so drunk he did not conceal
his contempt for strangers. A godsend
in the form of a reminder that I may not survive
the marriage. I walk on without direction.
Muslim families stare, failing to disguise
their amusement. Depression
wears a tight black dress and too much blush
while staggering beside a bin under stars,
a nobody without make-up and clothes—a hush
widens inside me at this thought. Cars
leaving the party drown out the sea.
The man I settled for is waiting for me.

Stern terns,
not gulls.
Good terms
or not,
they pose.
Imperious effigies.
An epithalamium.
Time's water
nudges them
lightly, unthinking.
And turn
to audit
each other
before divorcing.

How long does love like ours
tread water? Is our fighting
literal or littoral? Wordplay
what I fall back on
when nothing much else
convinces. There you go
whirling off into the sunset,
beachgoers casting us the side-eye.
Do I chase you—I will—
or might I rest my feet
in cool waters, dreaming of a cove
somewhere in Andromeda where nobody
is right or wrong, and nobody
predicts the hour our galaxies must clash?

Take the self
out of every
watery equation.
Wave after wave
the same wave
but, of course,
different. Believe
in disbelief.
Yourself. Myself.
Ourselves. If all
arguments
constituted an ocean—
how exhausting
when nothing stops.

Shy, shameful
shameplant or *Mimosa pudica*,
touch-me-not or maybe-
not-right-now, no shrinking violet
yet withdrawing nonetheless,
blinking shut bashfully
against prying fingers,
shutting it down temporarily
before unclasping
like eyes, purses, mini fans
or low to high tide
and possibly tsunami, longing
making lips or legs
unseal themselves and open.

Drugged out or deranged
from lockdown and high
on a nudity trend, Singaporeans
loitered naked at traffic junctions
armed with only a purse,
lay down flat on highways or
leapt over cars—why stop there?
Children of the pandemic
stripping away what cleaves us
to ourselves, we could stride
together clutching hands into what
beckons wetly on every side of the island.
I almost see our pixelated bodies
in the papers. The deep tilts us into itself.

What terrible lessons I teach myself
even now, said the universe
to itself in the body of the woman
bleeding out at the beach, stabbed
by an unknown stranger, how it would be
reported in newspapers tomorrow.
Some would say I have learnt
nothing at all in this interminable return
to form. The woman listens to retreating waves
and marvels at the moon's rheumy gash,
both of which are the universe mocking
itself. Where she was attacked will be regarded
as haunted, scaring visitors for decades to come.
But I am the ghost that never went away.

Slipping open sachets of you
under this voluminous tarp
of ocean without strangers
looking my way, day after day
after day, ashes, chunks,
stones that are all that is left
of you make their way away
from me and into the mouths
of fish, maybe even children
playing along the coast,
their parents yawning
to inhale before swimming
farther out to sea, your remains
bobbing like stars against the living.

Let us walk until we reach a restlessness
in every aspect. A longing for more
or less the same longing. Unmagnificent grandness
of a beach amassing leftovers from the sea floor.
Disagreement and conflict: crab and tern,
wave and sand, downpour and triumphant heat,
cyclist in the same manicured lane as pedestrian.
I argue that although incomplete,
passing harmonies stay longest in this country
here on the beach in our corner of evening
where men lock tongues under a tree.
Families have gone home. A guitar keeps playing.
Let us rest here on this bench and know
that rest is not eternal. A dead moon glows.

Contours, sloppy thresholds
of the unfinished, always
our great unfinished. Gates
of waves swinging shut
recede to open again.
Refractory promises of greater
completeness far beyond
this sandy sill. Apostates
amidst the din of self-
serving hustle, trespassing
where humans no longer tread,
swim or drown, we float on
until the mind is silent.
The sea wavers to deceive us.

After we die, we may walk this beach
forever. No toilet breaks. No hunger
beyond remembered hunger
for what we failed to renounce
as addiction and suffering. We could talk.
And talk. Dance across trees, walk on water—
walking keeps us humble.
Loss loses significance. Listening
is simultaneously music and empty score.
If duality bothered us before,
talking marries us here
to hereafter. No air without
rainfall without the day erasing our bodies.
Neither warm nor cold, you nor I.

Slumbering hull of this beach
pulses in the afterglow
of human activity. Unable
to determine where light
is growing from, no longer do you
feel alone. Or maybe the idea
of solitude is now
unnecessary. Like saying
the shore feels alone, or the sea.
Am I still here, listening?
Forgive me, I forget. I forgot
how distant we can be
over time. You the stirring world,
I the invisible sun rising.

I that is
not just the sun
but all things
flowing. Not
perfect, mind you:
imperfection
compels
discovery, like realizing
you cut your foot
underwater on a shell
angled to open
flesh. I that is
blood pearling out
from you like a question.

What keeps us
apart if not for chatter
that continues
as the rest of the country
bobs on the froth
of its own fake news?
You and I
the same duet
of being.
Sea and shore;
sea and swarming
sky. Clouds passing
into each other
slowly disappear.

What nocturne now? What scene?
Who sings while playing notes on a guitar,
crystalline with feeling (if not me)?
Who swims from here? Who gets left behind?
Whose whisper perseveres
like my own after the gloaming? Nobody
alone on the beach. Everybody
is alone. The passive-aggressive sea, again,
with its ear-licking commentary.
Non-self is not no-self, but selves
from waters we emerged
to mimic clouds lit by the moon behind them
hanging like a poem over our heads.
I pray to write it before falling into bed.

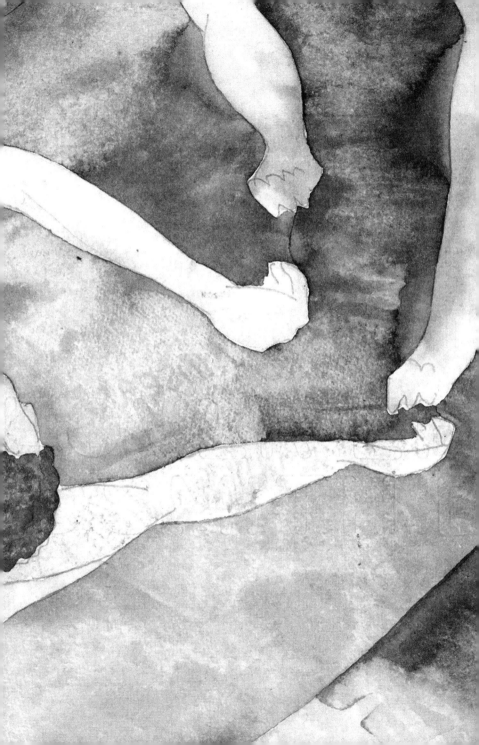